FLOWERS
FOR ALL SEASONS
SPRING

FLOWERS
FOR ALL SEASONS
SPRING

Text by Jane Packer and Elizabeth Wilhide

Fawcett Columbine · New York

Dedicated to Gary and "Ted"

A Fawcett Columbine Book
Published by Ballantine Books

Copyright © 1989 by Pavilion Books Limited

Published in Great Britain by Pavilion Books Limited.

Library of Congress Cataloging-in-Publication Data

Packer, Jane,1959-
Flowers for all seasons.
1. Flower arrangement. 2. Flowers. 3. Spring.
I. Title.
SB449.P223 1989   745.92   88-47891
ISBN: 0-449-90363-X

Printed and bound in Spain by Cayfosa Industria Grafica

First American Edition: February 1989

10 9 8 7 6 5 4 3 2 1

Contents

Introduction

In late December, it is very exciting to walk into the flower market and suddenly smell the heady scent which announces that the first narcissi have arrived. For me, after a couple of months of working with the rich reds and greens of Christmas, these pure white, bright yellow and orange flowers are particularly refreshing and welcome: true harbingers of spring.

By the end of any season, most people feel the need for a change and spring has particularly potent associations in this respect. Festivities such as St. Valentine's Day, Mother's Day and Easter all commemorate love and new life, antidotes to the grey days of winter.

Despite the increasing variety of flowers which is available all year round – thanks to commercial cultivation and imports – choosing flowers in season remains a worthwhile approach. First of all, it is a logical extension of the natural attitude to living which is so popular today, allowing you literally to bring the outdoors inside and express the mood of the time of year. It also means that you are obliged to change your ideas from time to time and exercise a little imagination to get around seasonal limitations: in this way you avoid stale, "foolproof" solutions and actually enjoy the flowers more. Lastly, the seasonal approach makes economic sense, which is especially important when creating large displays for weddings or special occasions. It is much easier, as well as cheaper, to base your ideas for an arrangement on what is readily available and in season than to pick a theme and then pay a fortune to realise it in flowers.

Each season has its own advantages and disadvantages. Spring flowers tend to be rather limited in terms of variety; they can be spare-looking and angular (which can be used to advantage); but their colours are fresh and light and they are often scented.

It is always better to work within these limitations, rather than against them. To create a natural landscape, for example, combine bare branches that are just beginning to bud with clusters of bulb flowers and moss, suggesting a spring garden where patches of bright colour suddenly appear among the new grass and dark earth. You can also supplement a few flowers with objects which have springtime associations, such as baskets, terracotta pots and eggs: arrangements do not have to consist of abundant cascades of flowers and foliage to be "natural" looking. Similarly, try to avoid colour themes for weddings or parties which are difficult to create in spring; opt for yellows or whites, rather than pinks, for example.

Above all, spring is a season for spontaneity and simplicity. Nothing could be easier than filling a jug with daffodils, but the cheerfulness of these flowers expresses the spring mood exactly.

JANE PACKER

Spring Flowers and Foliage

 When the first spring flowers begin to appear, it is a positive sign that winter is over. All of a sudden, tiny snowdrops pop up in the garden and before long there is the welcoming sight of crocuses and daffodils in the parks. After the dark months of rain and snow, it is no wonder that this is the season when people allow their hearts and senses free reign, and buy armfuls of flowers on impulse.

Flowers which are available during the spring months tend to share certain characteristics. Many are grown from bulbs and have thick, tubular stems, little foliage and simple, unpretentious flower heads. Colours are typically light and sunny, varying from pure white, through cream, to rich golden yellows. But this is also one time of the year when there is an excellent range of blues, from the deep mauve of miniature iris to the clear light blue of forget-me-nots. Yellow and blue, the spring colours, are naturally complementary, fresh-looking and cheerful.

Another important characteristic of spring flowers is their scent. Many are perfumed, which adds a special dimension to the enjoyment of bouquets and arrangements. The sweet smell of narcissi, the lovely fragrance of lily-of-the-valley or the fresh, fruity perfume of freesias heightens the sense of bringing the garden indoors.

Most spring flowers are relatively cheap. It is only if you want particularly long-stemmed varieties or a good display of foliage that price becomes more of an issue. Bulb flowers, however, are not particularly long-lasting when cut, and this can add to the expense of keeping fresh flowers constantly on display. Creating indoor gardens with potted flowers is one way of prolonging your enjoyment.

Right: A floor-level display of white tulips and hyacinths, simply arranged in a white jug and bowl. Tulips arc over as they age, growing towards the light. To arrange, gather all the heads together at the same height, place the flowers in the container and allow to fall naturally into place.

SELECTING FLOWERS

Buying in bud is particularly advisable for bulb flowers. Apart from one or two varieties of narcissi (Polaris or Soleil d'or) which can be bought fully open, it is better to select flowers which are still in bud to make the most of their short life. Avoid tight green buds which may never open and opt for those which are just beginning to show colour.

Always check any flowers wrapped in cellophane for signs of botrytis or mildew. Flowers which have been kept wrapped for several days will sweat because of the lack of ventilation and stems and foliage will begin to rot.

Foliage is a good indicator of health. This is especially true of potted azaleas. Wilted azalea flowers will revive readily after a soaking, but the leaves will remain hanging at an angle instead of their normal upright position.

SOURCES

A good florist is the best source for healthy fresh flowers and will stock a wider range of colours and varieties than the average market stall or corner shop. Shops which only carry flowers as a sideline – petrol stations, for example – may be less reliable. A lack of trained staff and a slower turnover of stock can lead to flowers being displayed when they are past their best.

Florists' flowers used to be synonymous with highly cultivated hothouse blooms, to the extent that when garden flowers became more commonly available in shops, people showed a certain reluctance to buy them. With fashion now swinging away from the formal and exotic in favour of natural effects, there is less of a distinction between what you can see growing in a garden and what is on sale in a flower shop. The biggest difference, which is particularly relevant in spring, is that many flowers appear much earlier in the flower shops than they do in the garden, by virtue of the flowers being commercially cultivated or flown in from warmer areas. And, of course, florists can supply many types of flower virtually all year round, which act as a useful supplement to the seasonal range.

Planning and planting a garden to create a source of cut flowers for the home is a subject in itself. But unless beds and borders are overflowing with blooms, most people have to compromise between having colour indoors or out. Although cutting annuals and perennials stimulates flower production, once a bulb flower is cut you will usually have to wait until the following year for it to appear in the garden again; you also rob the bulb of some of the nutrients it would have received if the foliage had been allowed to die down naturally. Cutting flowering shrubs or trees amounts to pruning; again there is the temptation to remove the most luxuriant branch for a display at the expense of the plant. Most gardens, however, can well stand a little cropping and home-grown flowers and foliage are especially satisfying.

Not only gardens, but also hedgerows, verges and neglected patches of land can provide plentiful sources of humble but attractive flowers and foliage, such as cow parsley (more commonly known in the United States as Queen Anne's lace) and ivy. Common meadow flowers such as buttercups and daisies always look charming and fresh. Aside from these common or invasive species, however, wild flowers should never be picked. Areas of true woodland, wild meadows and hedgerows are fast declining, with the loss of many species and it is important to leave the flowers and plants untouched to aid their conservation. Bluebells are one of the spring wild flowers which are now produced commercially, so there is no need to achieve a "wild" look with real wild flowers.

The Spring Palette

AMARYLLIS (*Hippeastrum* hybrids)
Availability Late winter through spring; cut or potted
Price Expensive if cut
Colour range White, apricot, pink, red
Life span Very long-lasting
Dramatic trumpet flowers on thick tubular stems; no foliage is available with cut flowers. Display full-length in see-through containers so that the stems are visible or cut short to feature the heads. Amaryllis heads are also useful in wedding arrangements and as bridal flowers.

ANEMONE (*Anemone coronaria*)
Availability Late winter through spring; cut
Price Cheap; long-stemmed varieties are more expensive
Colour range White, deep intense blue, red, purple
Life span Long-lasting
Good flower for mixed arrangements or on its own, with richer colours than typical spring shades. Very effective in low containers so that you can look down into the velvety centres. Spiky leaves clustered around each flower head.

AZALEA (*Rhododendron simsii*)
Availability December to spring; potted
Price Medium
Colour range Soft white, pale pink, deep shocking pink
Life span Long-lasting
Delicate furled fanlike flowers, single or double. Suit Japanese style modernity, as well as a more countrified look. When the plant has finished flowering, some varieties can be replanted as garden shrubs. Azaleas need a great deal of water. If the flowers wilt, plants in pots can be plunged under water until bubbles stop coming to the surface. The flowers will completely revive but leaves will remain flaccid and eventually drop if there has been a long delay between watering.

BLUEBELL (*Endymion hispanicus*)
Availability April; cut or potted (miniature)
Price Cheap
Colour range Blue, white
Life span Short life
Emphasize delicate appearance by arranging in small vases or mix with primroses for evocative springtime look. Avoid recutting if possible because of sap (p. 100). Will last longer in a vase, although stems are strong enough to use in oasis. Bluebells are slightly scented; avoid picking wild varieties.

BROOM (*Genesta*)
Availability March; cut
Price Expensive
Colour range Yellow (common garden variety), apricot, pale pink (commercial)
Life span Long-lasting
Flowering shrub which is available in garden or commercial varieties. The common garden variety is stiffer; commercial varieties are softer; both are highly scented. A sweeping arc of broom branches can be a useful way of extending the line of an arrangement; broom is also very effective displayed on its own for a stark, modern look. When the flowers have finished, foliage remains interesting and can be twisted, tied or bound.

CAMELLIA
Availability April, May; cut or potted
Price Expensive if cut
Colour range White, pinks, reds
Life span Long-lasting
Flowers bruise very easily; best displayed in arrangements. Dark, shiny leaves make very useful foliage, especially for wedding bouquets; fleshy leaves last well out of water. Crush woody stems to aid absorption of water.

CATKIN
Availability March, April; cut
Price Cheap
Colour range Yellow-green
Life span Long-lasting
These greeny-yellow tassels have a strong association with Easter and spring in general. Can be used on their own, mixed with other flowers to add sense of movement, or left to dry.

CLIVIA (Kaffir lily; *Clivia miniata*)
Availability March (cut) or as potted plant
Price Very expensive (cut); medium (potted)
Colour range Apricot
Life span Long-lasting
Thick tubular stem, with freesia-like flower at the top and thick glossy leaves. Use in a mixed arrangement as colour accent.

CORNFLOWER (Bachelor's buttons; *Centaurea cyanus*)
Availability Late spring; cut
Price Cheap
Colour range Characteristic blue, pink, white
Life span Short life
Small, round flower heads with wispy stems and foliage. Bright colour is a useful accent in mixed arrangements; display with grasses for a country meadow look. Simplicity of the flower means that it does not work particularly well in grand, formal arrangements.

COW PARSLEY/QUEEN ANNE'S LACE
Availability April; cut
Price Cheap; free if wild
Colour range White
Life span Lasts well
Fine, lacy flowers; grows naturally in neglected areas as a weed. Can be added to arrangement of white flowers as a filler or displayed on its own for a hazy, misty look. Florists stock long-stemmed white dill as an alternative; this is cheap with herby scent.

CROCUS (*Crocus* hybrids)
Availability Late December; potted
Price Cheap
Colours White, yellow, orange, blue
Life Long-lasting
These small brightly-coloured flowers are a traditional sign of spring. Mass pots in a basket for an indoor garden or combine with other potted bulbs.

DAFFODIL (*Narcissus* hybrids)
Availability From early October to end of May; cut
Price Cheap
Colour range White, cream, yellow, orange
Life span Long-lasting if kept in cool place
Daffodil is the common name for the larger narcissi; there are many different varieties from dainty miniatures to large double crowns. This cheerful, familiar flower often works best massed on its own for colour impact or in very simple mixtures, although there is a problem with sap (p. 100). Looks attractive in see-through vases so that stems are visible; difficult to use in oasis since stems will bend.

EUPHORBIA (Spurge; *Euphorbia fulgens*)
Availability Late spring; cut
Price Medium
Colour range White, pink, red, orange
Life span Long-lasting
Tiny flower clusters growing the length of the stem; extremely useful in mixed arrangements for extending the line of a display, adding height or a sense of movement. Many different varieties; flower-like green/yellow foliage.

FORGET-ME-NOT (*Myosotis alpestris*)
Availability April/May; cut or potted
Price Cheap
Colour range Blue or white
Life span Short life
Small dainty flowers, traditionally associated with weddings. Can be combined with other small flowers to make charming posies. Need to use in bunches to gain the impact of the colour. Stems are too frail for inserting in oasis unless you make the hole separately. Easily grown in garden, where they can be invasive.

FORSYTHIA (*Forsythia intermedia*)
Availability February; cut
Price Cheap
Colour range Yellow
Life span Very long-lasting
One of the most common flowering shrubs. Buy cut when just breaking into bud. Star-like yellow flowers on gnarled stems; good for modern displays with strong, graphic lines but too stiff to use readily in mixed arrangements.

FREESIA (*Freesia* hybrids)
Availability Year-round; cut or potted
Price Cheap to expensive
Colour range White, cream, pink, yellow, violet, blue, red
Life span Long-lasting
A popular wedding flower and a top seller, the freesia, especially the yellow variety, has a remarkable fruity smell which can permeate a room. Delicate, elongated sprays of single or double flowers; the more highly cultured and expensive have longer stems and come in single, rather than mixed colour bunches. Emphasize fragility by arranging freesias on their own in a simple glass vase. Can also be used in mixed arrangements or wedding bouquets.

FRUIT BLOSSOM (*Prunus* spp and *Malus* spp)
Availability December (commercially grown *Prunus*); April, May; cut
Price Cheap to expensive (early *Prunus*)
Colour range White, pink
Life span Long-lasting
Slightly scented clusters of blossoms from a range of ornamental fruit trees; commercially grown *Prunus* has a straight stem. Good for creating a Japanese-type display or for mixing with other flowers for country look. Cannot be used for wedding bouquets or headdresses since must be kept in water. Pink blossom will discolour water, so avoid see-through containers.

HYACINTH (*Hyacinthus orientalis* hybrids)
Availability December; cut or potted
Price Cheap
Colour range White, purple, blue, cream, apricot, pink
Life span Long-lasting
Popular, scented spring pot plant; miniature grape hyacinth (*Muscari*) also available. Combine with other potted bulbs for indoor garden; can also be used in mixed arrangements, but cut stems exude sap (see p. 100).

HYDRANGEA (*Hydrangea* spp)
Availability Late spring; potted
Price Varies according to quality
Colour range Blue, pink, white, cream
Life span Long-lasting
For best display, select plant with flat-topped spread of heads. Dainty "lace cap" variety makes a good instant display massed in pots, for a wedding or party. Can also be cut; crush stems to aid absorption of water. Dried hydrangeas are available in natural colours, bleached or dyed. Pot plants require constant watering.

IRIS (*Iris* spp)
Availability Year-round; January to March (miniature); cut or potted
Price Cheap
Colour range White, yellow, three shades of blue (*Iris xiphium* hybrids); deep mauve (miniature; *Iris reticulata*); green and black (widow iris; *Hermodactylus tuberosus*)
Life span Long-lasting if potted
Popular, ubiquitous cut flower. Useful source of blue in mixed arrangements; suits formal display, tall cylindrical containers. Miniature is delicate, and scented; widow iris intriguingly exotic.

IVY (*Hedera* sp)
Availability Year-round; cut or potted
Colour range Greens, yellow, white (variegated)
Price Cheap
Life span Long-lasting
Readily available and versatile foliage, more natural-looking than traditional florist's foliage. Great variety of size, leaf shape and colour. Strong leaves can be wired for use in bouquets and will stand up well; good at conveying a sense of movement. In arrangements, ivy helps to extend the lines so that displays trail away rather than having stiff blunt ends.

JASMINE (*Jasminum* sp)
Availability Winter through to spring; potted
Price Expensive
Colour range White, yellow, pink-tinged
Life span Long-lasting
Delicate, scented star-like flowers on arcing stem. Potted plants can be cut to use in wedding bouquets or arrangements, as trails or tendrils. A little sparse to be displayed on its own. Outdoor-grown jasmine, flowering later in the summer, looks stronger, with heavier flower clusters.

LILAC (*Syringa* spp)
Availability Late winter (forced); April, May; cut
Price Very expensive (early) to medium
Colour range White, pink, lilac, deep purple
Life span Long-lasting
Beautifully scented flowering shrub, with clusters of tiny flowers. Used in mixed arrangements or on its own in vases, but not in see-through containers as the water quickly discolours. Good foliage, but does not last as long as the flowers; foliage can be removed when it has wilted. Split or crush the woody stems to aid absorption of water.

LILY (*Lilium spp*)
Availability Year-round (cut); late spring to summer (potted)
Price Expensive
Colour range All colours except blue
Life span Long-lasting
There are many different varieties of this elegant flower but the green or white arum lily and the trumpet-shaped longiflorum lilies are particularly associated with spring and Easter festivities. Although expensive, one lily can look elegant displayed on its own in a fluted vase. Fragrant; remove pollen heads to avoid staining clothing. Traditional symbol of purity; popular choice for wedding arrangements; also suits chic modern interiors.

LILY-OF-THE-VALLEY (*Convallaria majalis*)
Availability Year-round; cut
Price Expensive
Colour range White
Life span Long-lasting
Popular wedding flower; heady perfume, delicate white bells and wonderful glossy leaves. Mix with other white flowers or mass in a low container, overspilling the sides so the bells are visible. Traditional May Day gift in France.

MAGNOLIA (*Magnolia* spp)
Availability April; cut
Colour range Pure white, "magnolia" white, pink
through purple
Price Expensive
Life span Long-lasting
Gardens are often a better source than florists. Waxy flower
from tulip-sized down to small star, depending on variety.
Good foliage; preserved leaves are readily available. Flower
can be used in wedding work; branches are stunning dis-
played on their own.

MARIGOLD (*Tagetes* spp)
Availability March to July; cut
Price Cheap
Colour range Acid yellow, bright orange, dark orange
Life span Short life
Although marigolds are a summer bedding plant, they are
commercially available much earlier. Can be cut low to mass
into a bowl for vivid colour; used as colour accent in mixed
arrangements. Not a subtle flower, so unsuitable for a classical
formal display.

MIMOSA (*Mimosa* spp)
Availability December to March; cut
Colour range Yellow
Price Expensive
Life span Short life
Perfumed; sprays of tiny, fluffy balls of blossom massed on
stem; use on its own or in mixed arrangements.

MOSS (various species)
Availability Year-round
Price Cheap
Colour range Pale to dark green
Life span Long-lasting
Useful surface covering for planted arrangements; gives
textural interest combined with baskets; conceals fixing points.
Two main varieties available commercially: bun moss, which is
velvety green, and sphagnum moss, with springier, shorter
fibres. Sphagnum moss can be used to cover the base of a
wreath or garland.

NARCISSUS (*Narcissus* hybrids)
Availability December to March; cut or potted
Price Expensive (early) to cheap (late)
Colour range White, yellow, peach
Life span Short life
There are hundreds of varieties, from the very tiny ("Cheerfulness"), to those almost as big as daffodils. Narcissi are
generally distinguished from daffodils by shortness of their
centre trumpets. Most are very highly scented. Suit casual,
informal arrangements; mass different varieties or mix with
daffodils. Stems exude sap (see p. 100).

PANSY (*Viola wittrockiana*)
Availability April (commercially grown); potted
Price Cheap
Colour range All shades from white to black
Life span Last well in pots; only one day if cut
Characteristic velvety faces, rich colours, delicate stems. Can
be perfumed. Best way of displaying is by grouping pots in
baskets, surrounded by moss.

PRIMROSE (*Primula* spp)
Availability Late December to March; cut or potted
Price Cheap (potted) to expensive
Colour range "Primrose" yellow, violet, pink
Life span Short life
Low spreading leaves and delicate petalled flowers. Charming
in posies or simple arrangements. Use potted plants in indoor
gardens; when the flowers have finished, can be planted out in
the garden.

RANUNCULUS (*Ranunculus asiaticus*)
Availability October to May; cut
Price Expensive (early) to cheap
Colour range White, cream, pink, yellow, red
Life span Long-lasting
Available in mixed or single-colour bunches (which tend to be
more expensive). Frilly petals, uncultivated look; versatile in
arrangements. Heads tend to hang, so good at suggesting a
sense of movement.

ROSE (miniature) (*Rosa* sp)
Availability Year-round; cut
Price Expensive
Colour range White, pink, red, yellow
Life span Long-lasting
Extremely versatile flower for arrangements, bouquets, vases or even combined with food. Trim base of stems at angle; the longer the stem the deeper the water must be. If the heads drop and fail to open, put the stems in two inches of boiling water for twenty seconds to clear any airblocks, wrap tightly in newspaper and put in deep water for two hours.

SNOWDROP (*Galanthus nivalis*)
Availability December to February; cut or potted
Price Cheap
Colour range White
Life span Short life
Very simple, fresh and dainty flower, often the first sign of spring. Display on its own in a simple container.

SOLOMON'S SEAL (*Polygonatum x hybridum*)
Availability April (2-3 weeks); cut
Price Cheap
Colour range White
Life span Long-lasting
Bright emerald green arc of leaves with little white bells underneath; once popular in Victorian walled gardens. Needs to be displayed so that both aspects are visible – at eye level or above. Sweeping curve gives fluidity to arrangements; not suitable for wired wedding bouquets. Bells die first, but foliage lasts well.

SPIRAEA (*Spiraea* spp)
Availability April to late summer
Colour range White, pale pink, purple; leaves can be variegated
Price Medium
Life span Long-lasting
Flowering shrub with arc-like branch and hazy flowers. Use within mixed arrangements.

STOCK (*Matthiola incana*)
Availability Late spring; cut
Price Medium
Colour range White, cream, pink, lilac, purple
Life span Short life
Lush foliage; a single bunch can look abundant. Heavy scent. Remove foliage below the water line and change water daily.

VIOLET (*Viola* spp)
Availability February, March; cut or potted
Price Cheap
Colour range White, purple (cut)
Life span Long-lasting
Traditional flower for posy, in tied bunches with ivy or violet leaves. Too small for a big arrangement but can be massed in a low bowl. Potted violets make good gifts for Mother's Day or birthdays. If cut violets begin to wilt, completely submerge flowers and stems in water for 15 to 30 minutes and they will revive.

WALLFLOWER (*Cheiranthus cheiri*)
Availability Throughout spring; cut
Price Cheap
Colour range Rich reds, yellows, deep pinks
Life span Long-lasting
Common garden flower which is sometimes overlooked because of familiarity. Long stems, perfumed; can be used in grand, formal arrangements; good depth of colour.

YEAR-ROUND FLOWERS
Although some of the following flowers and foliage are associated with a particular season, they are generally available year-round from florists and flower stalls, and make a useful supplement to the typical seasonal range.
*indicates description in text

ALSTROEMERIA	GYPSOPHILA
BOX	*IRIS
CARNATION	*IVY
CHRYSANTHEMUM	LAUREL
CUPRESSUS	*LILY
EUCALYPTUS	*MOSS
*FREESIA	ORCHID
GLADIOLI	*ROSE

TULIP (*Tulipa* hybrids)
Availability November to June; cut
Price Cheap in season
Colour range All shades from white through deep purple; striped
Life span Long-lasting
There are many different varieties, including double tulips, miniature tulips, and parrot tulips with serrated, frilly petals. Good at providing a block of strong colour; suits modern, simple vases. Equally effective in mixed displays. Tulips are the only flower that continues to grow once cut, until the head becomes too heavy for the stem and flops down. Can exploit this tendency by placing at edge of arrangement for a flowing line. If the tulips become limp, roll in a tube of paper and leave for two hours in deep water.

A Style for Spring

Unlike summer, spring is not a season which teams with rich colours, lush, abundant foliage or a profusion of varieties. Although it is perfectly possible, and it may be tempting, to sidestep such limitations by making use of imported or commercial flowers, it is often a better strategy just to accept them and enjoy this brief season for its own qualities. The innate simplicity and delicacy of spring flowers makes a welcome and refreshing start to the year. Whites, yellows and clear blues are all colours which immediately lighten and brighten a room. A pot of primroses brings a touch of sunshine to a dull grey day; cool, blue hyacinths are refreshing; dainty snowdrops and lily-of-the-valley have a delicate, fragile charm. The lack of foliage and short stems mean that small-scale arrangements often work best.

But the cheapness of many spring flowers, especially bulbs, allow flowers to be massed in bunches for greater impact. Stems can be left visible in see-through containers; their bright, fresh green is naturally complementary. Displays which incorporate potted flowers not only prolong the short life of many of these varieties but also look appropriately charming and unpretentious.

Above left: Massed grape hyacinths and lily-of-the-valley pick up the blue and white of the Chinese jug. Colours are kept separate rather than intermingled to add impact. Bunches are left secured with elastic bands, to maintain a sense of fullness.

Right: To make the most of a few flowers or display a beautiful container, you can adopt an asymmetrical arrangement, laying flowers cut short on the rim. Hydrangea, pale blue hyacinths, pink parrot tulips and jasmine trails echo the soft colours of the bowl. The arrangement needs to be viewed from above.

FLOWERS FOR THE HOME

Flower arrangements for everyday enjoyment should be quite different from those you create for a special occasion. Primarily they should look at ease in their surroundings, complementing colours and mood. They should also be a natural extension of your tastes and preferences. In the past, a flower arrangement all too often tended to mean a stiff, formal construction placed prominently in a room, as if an important event was just about to happen. Nowadays, most people prefer displays to look natural and uncontrived; they want flowers to appear a permanent part of their lifestyle, even if that is not always the case. In spring the tendency is toward the informal and unsophisticated and as long as you go along with this feeling there is less risk of creating an inappropriately formal or grand effect.

But if the overriding aim is informality and naturalness, there is also a need for flowers to be noticed. Whether the intention is to draw attention to a fine feature such as a collection of china or a painting, or to distract the eye from some less-than-perfect element, flowers have to be chosen, arranged and positioned with care, so that they are most effective and you can derive the maximum pleasure from them. It is important to get the balance right – flowers should not be dominant and overpowering, but neither should they be insignificant.

Left: Yellow tulips and ranunculus tone with the cream background of a classical alcove. The terracotta pots and variation in height strike a note of informality.

Right: Responding to the silvery colours of the setting – in particular the pewter side table – this low arrangement consists of white amaryllis, bluebells, and blue and white anemones, together with cuttings of budding foliage: a shimmering spring look.

Above: White arum lilies often suggest elegant arrangements, but they can be equally effective used in a more informal way. The plain enamel jug makes a suitably upright container; white rhubarb flowers and bare twigs add fullness to the display.

Left: Unusual containers always add life to an arrangement. Here the dainty, facetted glass of an antique inkstand makes the perfect foil for a simple display of lily-of-the-valley. Ivy adds a depth of colour. Ivy is invaluable in Spring, when the range of foliage is limited.

COLOUR

One of the simplest ways of choosing flowers for indoors is by colour. Flowers can provide a striking accent, enhance an existing scheme by coordinating with the colours of rugs, upholstery, curtain fabric or paintings, and even underline a particular style or mood. Certain species such as tulips – which are available in almost every colour – as well as the rich deep shades of anemones can be a useful supplement to the light, sunny spring palette.

Tulips are particularly effective in stark, modern rooms, where they provide a splash of colour and vitality. The orangey yellow and fresh sharp green of daffodils is a perfect accompaniment to Art Deco style. In a period room, an arrangement of different white flowers can look supremely elegant. For a more informal, country look, you can mix as many colours as possible to suggest a flowering meadow.

Left: Daffodils epitomize spring, but their stiff tubular stems can limit their potential for arrangement. The sweeping curve of broom and variegated ivy trails help to break this strong upright line, while primroses coordinate with the two varieties of daffodil.

Right: Broken camellia heads, which might otherwise be discarded, are floated in a bowl of water. Although this type of display will only last for a short while, it makes a highly effective centrepiece.

POSITION

Practically speaking, most spring flowers benefit from being kept in a cool environment, where they will last a little while longer, so try to avoid placing flowers on south-facing window sills, on mantelpieces if fires are still being lit, on kitchen counters near ovens or hobs, and in steamy bathrooms. The hallway is a good location for an arrangement, not only because flowers are a welcoming sight for visitors but also because the temperature tends to be lower.

The proportion and scale of a room is an important consideration. A tiny display on a mantelpiece will be dwarfed by a high ceiling; a tumbling cascade of flowers on a small side table will look top-heavy and over-powering. Arrangements should also be positioned well away from traffic routes. It is uncomfortable to worry constantly that a vase might be upset.

The key to positioning flowers is eyeline. Fireplaces are natural focal points and mantelpieces make good locations for displays that can be viewed from standing height – as you enter the room, for example. But upright bulb flowers such as daffodils are rather wasted on a high mantelpiece, since they do not offer much interest when seen from below. Tulips, which curl downwards as they age, would be a better choice, making a good display from a standing or sitting viewpoint. In the same way, low-level arrangements on coffee tables, floors or hearths should be designed so you can look into the flower heads, by cutting the stems of larger flowers such as lilies or amaryllis short or grouping together smaller flowers such as primroses or forget-me-nots. On side tables, you can arrange collections of containers of different heights for variety; positioning flowers in front of a mirror will multiply the view.

CONTAINERS

Containers can do a great deal to alter the appearance of a flower, both in terms of scale and shape, and in terms of style. Straight glass cylinders or ceramic vases suit modern decor and are a good way of displaying bold upright flowers such as daffodils, tulips and irises.

Right: Orange double tulips are massed in a shining copper trough in a simple and unpretentious display. The tulips are planted directly in the container. Twigs bound round the base of the stems support the flowers as they grow; moss is laid on top of the earth.

Overleaf: A subtle coordination of flowers and fabric pattern is achieved using peach parrot tulips, clivia cut from a plant, apricot hyacinths and narcissi, all arranged in a soft turquoise vase. The round ball of flowers echoes the shape of the container.

More of a country look can be achieved by using earthenware bowls, terracotta pots or patterned ceramics. The fragility of bluebell or freesia stems can be emphasized by delicate clear containers, such as Victorian wine glasses or old perfume bottles.

Baskets are especially evocative of Easter and Mother's Day, particularly when filled with small dainty flowers such as narcissi and forget-me-nots. There is a wide range available, from fine painted wicker to the more overtly rustic, woven from coarse grasses, vines and even dried roots and herbs. Baskets can be waterproofed by lining them with plastic bags and then planted; alternatively, water-filled jam jars can be concealed inside for cut flower arrangements.

Remember that you do not have to search for a tall vase to suit long-stemmed flowers; the stems can always be cut, which might even increase the life of the flowers. Narrow necked containers will hold fine stems in position, but wide-necked ones can be adapted by using a chicken wire or tape grid (see p. 107). Plastic florist's trays, saucers or plates all make suitable reservoirs for oasis.

TYPES OF ARRANGEMENT

Traditional floristry, with its rules of proportion, angles of construction and emphasis on achieving formal, symmetrical shapes, has acquired a reputation for being unsympathetic and artificial. This is somewhat of a misrepresentation — many of these rules are based on common sense. But today it is possible to avoid a contrived look, achieve a sense of naturalness and spontaneity while still benefiting from the florist's skills and techniques: it is not necessary to renounce the use of chicken wire, foam, water vials or any other tools of the trade which help to extend the creative scope.

To create natural-looking arrangements it is important, first of all, to observe how flowers really grow. If you step out into a garden, you will not see flowers arranged in neat triangular shapes or Hogarthian curves. You will see clusters of species growing together, sprays of flowers and buds, tiny new growth tapering away at the

Right: Spring offers a wide variety of blues: crocus, hyacinth, grape hyacinth, bluebells, iris, anemones and forget-me-nots. This cottage-style arrangement of grape hyacinths, hyacinths and anemones in a vivid blue jug accentuates the intense colour of a butterfly collection.

end of a branch or edge of a border. In spring, the habit of growth is sparse and low. Daffodils and tulips wave on straight stems; there are low clumps of snowdrops, crocuses and primroses, and drifts of bluebells in the woodlands. To recreate this sense of the spring garden or landscape, cluster species together. You do not need to use a great deal of flowers — a few blooms interspersed with moss and pebbles will suggest a flowering lawn. If you want a curving, flowing shape, exploit those flowers which arc naturally, such as tulips, which flop over as they age, Solomon's seal, jasmine or trails of ivy. Stiff, blunt edges are unknown in nature: place the larger flowers at the centre, the smaller ones towards the edge and use delicate flowers to break up the line and soften the edges.

Many traditional notions are worth consideration. One useful rule-of-thumb is to allow one-and-a-half times the height of flowers to container. Visually, this obviously makes sense — a top-heavy arrangement looks awkward, while a tiny margin of flowers at the top means that you see more container than flower. But there are other reasons for this basic proportion — long-stemmed flowers in a short container are easily upset and the water has so far to travel that the flowers have little chance of getting the nourishment they need. A classic mistake is to buy expensive long-stemmed roses and then expect them to survive in 8 or 9 inches (20cm or so) of water. On the other hand, if you want to create a low arrangement, where you can look down into the flower heads, the stems can be cut very short so that the flower stands only about 2 inches (5 cm) above the bowl. Rules are made to be broken, of course. Clean-lined blooms such as daffodils or tulips can very effectively be displayed in a tall glass vase with not much more than their heads above the rim; the stems will form part of the display and avoid an unbalanced look.

Another idea is to combine flowers in odd numbers in front-facing or triangular arrangements. Working in threes, fives, sevens makes good visual sense — it avoids the static, regimented look that balanced compositions of even numbers sometimes produce.

Left: This predominantly green display was designed so as not to detract from the trompe l'oeil *painting or garden view. Arranged in oasis, in sections to suggest a landscape, are several large hogweed leaves, some silvery florist's foliage, three white tulips just beginning to open and a white primula plant.*

Narcissi Tree

Since narcissi are among the cheapest and most readily available of all spring flowers you can buy several bunches, rather than just one, and mass the flowers to increase their impact. Narcissi flower heads are fairly flat, which means they can be bunched tightly. This tree shape, created for a child's room, makes a feature of both massed stems and heads – an unusual and amusing treatment for one of the common sights of spring.

FLOWERS AND FOLIAGE

Several bunches of Bridal Crown narcissi (a double-flowered variety)
A narcissus leaf

MATERIALS

Glass tank container with convex base
Double-sided tape
Twine

METHOD

1 Bunch the flowers tightly together in one hand, massing the flower heads. Tie the stems with twine.
2 Wrap a narcissus leaf around the stems to cover the twine. Either knot in place or secure with small pieces of double-sided tape.
3 Cut the stems level. Stand the tree in the tank, splaying out the stems so that the tree stands upright.

CARE

Change the water daily if possible. This arrangement will last about four days if kept in a fairly cool place.

In the Pink

An easy way to combine different varieties of flower is to coordinate them by colour. Cut low into a wide bowl, and softened by foliage, these flower heads make a pretty pink display which here complements the simple wicker furniture. A potted azalea adds fullness to the arrangement – a useful way of filling a large container and a perfectly acceptable "cheat".

FLOWERS AND FOLIAGE

Potted azalea
Hyacinths
Tulips
Parrot tulips
Single amaryllis
Cow parsley/Queen Anne's Lace
Tulip leaves

MATERIALS

Low wide bowl
Brick or plastic lining

METHOD

1   Fill the bowl with water and place the potted azalea in it to one side. Rest the pot on a brick to keep it clear of the water, or wrap the pot in a plastic lining so that the plant does not become waterlogged.
2   Cut the foliage and cow parsley/Queen Anne's Lace so that 2 inches (5 cm) protrude above the bowl. Arrange foliage in the bowl, working from the edges to the centre.
3   Cut the flowers low and balance in the foliage, again working from the edges to the centre. Group species together, with tulips splaying over the edge and larger, taller flowers building height at the centre.

CARE

Water the azalea frequently; change the water in the container as necessary. Flowers will last about a week; the pot plant will carry on flowering.

Fireside Glow

Marigolds are plentiful, vivid and fun to use in bold, cheerful displays. Flanked by helxine plants (baby's tears, *Soleirolia*) and echoing their rounded shape, a dome of marigolds is massed in the grate, making a blaze of colour that adds warmth to a plain modern hearth. Three terracotta pots are lined up in front, each carrying a ball of flowers.

FLOWERS AND FOLIAGE

Marigolds and marigold leaves
Two potted helxines

MATERIALS

Low plastic trough
Three terracotta pots
Oasis
Polythene lining

METHOD

1   Line the pots with polythene. Insert a square of soaked oasis into each pot, so that the oasis protrudes above the rim.
2   Cut the marigolds short and insert into the oasis, making a dome of flower heads. Add a few leaves for contrast.
3   Fill a low plastic trough with water and place in the grate. Mass marigolds in the trough, adding leaves for contrast.
4   Flank the display with helxine plants.

CARE

The marigolds in water will last slightly longer than those in oasis – about one week.

Woodland Arrangement

Now that bluebells are available commercially, it is possible to bring indoors the beauty of the woodlands in spring. Because bluebell stems are too frail and fine for oasis, other means must be devised to hold the flowers in place. Here a grid of tape across the neck of the container fulfils this function; moss laid on top acts as a disguise. The same method could be applied to narrow the neck of any wide container.

FLOWERS AND FOLIAGE

Bluebells
Bun moss

MATERIALS

Glass vase
Tape

METHOD

1   Lay strips of tape across the neck of the vase to form a grid. (A glass vase is preferable so that the stems remain visible.)
2   Insert the bluebells in the centre square.
3   Lay moss across on top of the tape to hide the grid.

CARE

Change the water, daily, if possible. This display will last five to six days.

Elegant Simplicity

A marble-topped table and gilt mirror make a grand setting for a simple horizontal arrangement of spring flowers and moss; the flowing line of the display does not obscure the view of the mirror or compete with the rich background. The flowers are selected to echo the golden colours of the marble and gilt, and dotted in small, sparse groups to suggest natural growth. This type of arrangement is a good way of making the most of a few flowers.

FLOWERS AND FOLIAGE

Pansies
Ranunculus
Narcissi
Willow twig
Ivy
Bun moss
Sphagnum moss

MATERIALS

Low saucer or plate
Oasis
Wire or hairpins

METHOD

1 Place a square of soaked oasis on a plate or saucer.
2 Start in the centre, inserting groups of tall flowers to create height.
3 Insert small clusters of flowers at the sides to extend the line horizontally.
4 To simulate a natural landscape and to hide the oasis, pin moss around the flower clumps using wire or hairpins.
5 Add the willow twig and ivy trails to soften the edges of the arrangement.

CARE

Water daily.

Pot-et-Fleur

In this updated version of the traditional *pot-et-fleur* arrangement, which combines living with cut flowers, the old-fashioned charm of pansies and trails of jasmine create the right country look for a period bedroom, with its painted chest-of-drawers and floral drapery. The *pot-et-fleur* format is a good way of dressing up hothouse plants.

FLOWERS AND FOLIAGE

Potted early pansies (brought on in the greenhouse)
Jasmine, cut from a pot plant
Moss

MATERIALS

Small rustic basket
Florist's vial or test tube
Wire or hairpins
Plastic lining

METHOD

1   Line the basket with plastic.
2   Tuck the pot of pansies into the basket.
3   Insert a vial of water into the soil in the pot. Place the cut end of the jasmine in the vial. Arrange the jasmine so that it flows around the side of the basket.
4   Pin moss around the top of the basket to disguise the rim of the pot.

CARE

Water the pansies in the pot. Check the water level in the vial regularly.

Water Garden

Especially if a container is itself worthy of attention, there is no need to fill it up with flowers. This green crackle-glazed bowl inspired an off-centre arrangement of lily-of-the-valley and narcissi. The display gains impact by using the minimum of flowers and is a way of appreciating both their delicacy and the beauty of the bowl.

FLOWERS AND FOLIAGE

White narcissi
Lily-of-the-valley, with leaves
Ivy

MATERIALS

Shallow bowl
Twine or elastic band

METHOD

1   Gather the narcissi into a flat rosette and bind together with some twine or an elastic band. Cut the stems short.
2   Position the rosette so the stems are resting in water.
3   Tuck the stems of the lily-of-the-valley, the leaves and ivy under the rosette, so that the narcissi stems are hidden.

CARE

Because the flowers are resting so near the water, this display will only last about three days.

Primrose Basket

Spring flowers such as primroses are often simple and dainty and best displayed in unpretentious, informal arrangements that suggest the garden rather than the hothouse. Many also have fine, short stems which are difficult to use in oasis. This low basket display would also be a good solution for other short-stemmed spring flowers, such as violets, snowdrops or anemones. It should be positioned on a low table so it can be viewed from above.

FLOWERS AND FOLIAGE

Bunches of primroses
Variegated ivy, Gold Child or similar

MATERIALS

Rustic basket
Bowl
Twine

METHOD

1   Fill the bowl with water and place it in the basket.
2   Mass the primroses in the bowl, leaving them in twined bunches.
3   Add the ivy, placing the cut end in the water. This particular variety of ivy has a golden tinge to the variegation, which coordinates with the green and yellow of the primroses.

CARE

Change the water daily, if possible. The display will last about a week.

Spring Garden

An excellent way of displaying spring flowers is in a planted arrangement, which not only looks delightful and natural, but lasts much longer than cut flowers. Lending a certain rustic charm to a riverside breakfast table, this garden could be expected to last three to four weeks.

FLOWERS AND FOLIAGE

Potted miniature daffodils
Cut primroses
Potted muscari
Potted forget-me-nots
Potted variegated ivy
Bun moss

MATERIALS

Large rustic basket
Plastic lining
Potting compost
Broken crockery or stones
Pebbles
Hairpins or fine wire
Test tube or florist's vial

METHOD

1　Line the basket with plastic lining and cover the bottom with a layer of broken crockery or stones. Fill with potting compost.
2　Plant out the flowers in asymmetrical groupings, clustering the same species together, as they would grow naturally. To emphasize the landscape effect, place the taller plants at the back.
3　Plant the ivy to one side, allowing it to overflow the side of the basket. "Plant" the primroses in a test tube or vial filled with water, embedded in the soil.
4　Surround the flowers with pebbles and bun moss laid directly on the top.
5　Tuck a few pieces of moss into the wicker at the side of the basket and secure with hairpins or fine wire.

CARE

It is important not to over-water because of lack of drainage. Keep in a fairly cool place. Baskets lined with plastic need careful watering to avoid leakage.

Spring Weddings

The date of a wedding is generally chosen with great care. Sometimes the day has a special association, marking a family anniversary or tradition. Less specifically the bride may just have a vague notion that she would prefer to be married in a particular season. Whatever the reason, it is especially effective (not to mention economical) to choose wedding flowers that evoke the time of year. Appropriately seasonal flowers provide a built-in theme which gives a special unity and atmosphere to the entire day.

Spring flowers are ideal for wedding displays. Many of the locations where weddings are celebrated, such as churches or synagogues, are dimly lit and the fresh appearance of these naturally light and sunny flowers helps to brighten up the dark corners. White flowers are always a popular choice for weddings and spring provides a wealth of different whites and creams to suit any colour scheme or dress fabric. Spring days are also notoriously unpredictable; if the day turns out to be cool and cloudy, sunny yellow flowers will add a welcome touch of warmth. If the wedding is to take place on a special day such as St. Valentine's Day, the first day of spring or Easter, the occasion can be given additional emphasis by the choice of flowers many of which are scented, which further adds to the beauty of the day.

Above left: Pink peonies (an early import) make a supremely feminine bouquet, softened by sprays of gypsophila, one of the most popular of all wedding flowers.

Right: As many spring flowers wilt early, wedding varieties must be chosen with care so that they survive the day. It is better to rely on cultured flowers which have been grown for their lasting qualities. Lilac, jasmine, roses, sweetpeas and lily-of-the- valley, all perfumed, have been used in both the bouquet and headdress.

Left: The entrance hall is a good place for a welcoming display of flowers. The table centrepiece consists of a mixture of euphorbia, primula and white lilac, with jasmine trails and lilac leaves, all assembled in a low bowl. The foreground posy is a wired asymmetric bouquet of white lilac, bound and tied with lace.

CHOOSING WEDDING FLOWERS

In any season, bridal flowers need to be chosen with careful thought to their lifespan. Certain flowers, no matter how appropriate or personally meaningful, will simply not last well in bouquets or headdresses, especially if they are wired. A bouquet can take an hour and a half to make and must often be delivered to the bride at least two hours before the wedding so that there is enough time for the hairdresser and photographer to do their work. This means that by the time the wedding party is ready for the ceremony, the flowers will have already been out of water for nearly four hours.

In general, fleshier flowers and foliage that hold liquid well will survive best. Unfortunately, the fresh light green of spring foliage is often ruled out – the new growth is usually too soft to hold up well all day. Narcissi and daffodils also do not last well in bouquets but are perfectly suitable for church or reception arrangements. The bouquet can be coordinated with these displays by choosing, say, roses in the same colours.

SUITABLE SPRING FLOWERS AND FOLIAGE

Amaryllis   Large trumpet flowers provide good strong focal points in bouquets.

Anemones   Vivid colours and natural appeal. Difficult to use in wired bouquets. If you do need to wire, wrap stems in damp cotton first to hold in moisture.

Carnations   Good range of colours. Although the flowers are bulky, you can split or "shatter" the heads and wire three or four petals together. Traditional buttonhole for groom and ushers.

Catkins   Good at providing a sense of movement in bouquets.

Chrysanthemums   Single varieties have a country look in mixed tied bunches. Good soft creams and whites.

Cyclamen leaves   Sturdy dark leaf which is very useful in bouquets.

Forget-me-nots   Charming in tied posies. Traditional source of "something blue".

Freesias   Very popular wedding flower with splendid scent, wide range of colours and delicate appearance.

Gardenias   Beautifully scented white flower; cut from pot plants.

Gladioli   Although the whole flower spike would be too dominant for a bouquet, florets wired individually can be very effective.

Gypsophila   Popular frothy white or pink flowers give a hazy effect.

Hyacinths   Good colour range and scent. Individual bells can be wired into bouquets.

Ivy   Strong, well-defined leaf, excellent for bouquets. Trails of ivy add a sense of movement. Symbolizes fidelity and the "lasting bond of marriage".

Jasmine   Like ivy, a way of softening the line of a bouquet.

Lilac   White variety has a fresh green tint; scented.

Lilies   Excellent wedding flower despite the unfortunately persistent association with funerals.

Lily-of-the-valley   One of the most popular bridal flowers. Delicate scented bells good for trailing lines. Dark glossy leaves also work well in bouquets.

Muscari   Grape hyacinths are another good source of blue.

Orchids   Suitable for formal, dramatic bouquets. Some varieties, such as Cymbidium can look heavy; mix with daintier Singapore orchids to soften the effect.

Roses   Invaluable wedding flowers; good colour range, scent and life.

Tulips   Good at providing colour. Pure white and pastels as well as stronger shades.

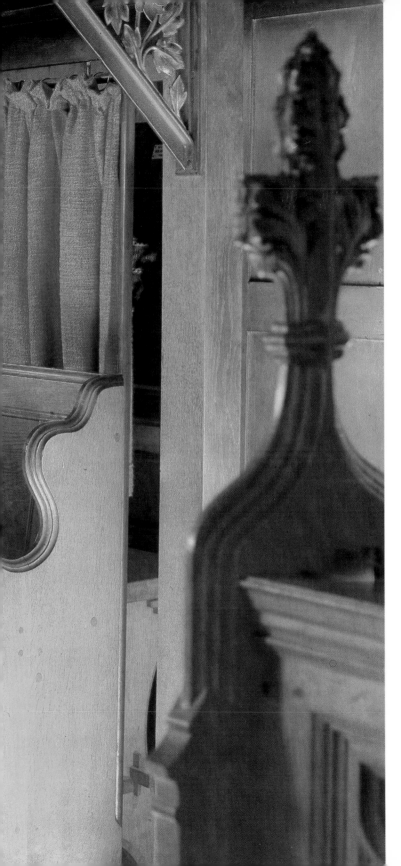

Above: The central candelabra supports a basket carrying bunches of white narcissi and violets, spilling over the sides. Colours are kept separate to maximize impact.

Left: Wherever a wedding is celebrated, flower decorations should be bold enough to read well from a distance. This choir stall display was designed to look overgrown and trailing. A rope of bun moss (bound in with string) winds along the stall and up the bases of the candelsticks. Onto the rope are pinned baskets filled with violets, miniature white roses, lily-of-the-valley and yellow euphorbia. Cow parsley and ivy soften the lines and add to the natural effect.

Above: A full-skirted wedding dress needs to be complemented by a large, full bouquet to balance the entire effect. Foliage trails add an important sense of movement: a bouquet should never be rigid and stiff.

Opposite: Architectural details can inspire floral designs. A deep picture rail provides enough room for shallow containers which carry large blocks of oasis. Clumps of five or six narcissi and daffodil heads are used together so that they remain visible from a distance and foliage is trailed down and across the arch. The central rosette consists of a tightly bunched posy of narcissi, ringed with ivy leaves.

THE BRIDE'S FLOWERS

The bride will be the focus of attention throughout the day. Her flowers – bouquet and headdress – should be considered first and can provide the colour or style upon which the other displays are based.

It is important not to plan too far ahead. Only when the dresses for the bride and her attendants have been chosen can you begin to make firm decisions about the flowers. It is always a good idea for both the florist and bride to be able to proceed with one plan rather than have to change ideas several times along the way.

You should begin with an overall impression of the bride, her colouring, height and size. Blue flowers, for example, suit fair skins better than they do olive complexions. Avoid trailing bouquets if the bride is short. Similarly, a tiny posy will look slightly absurd carried by the statuesque.

The dress is also an important factor. A simple style in broderie anglaise, for example, can be accentuated by a dainty, country-style bouquet; a silk gown will demand more refinement. A full-skirted ball gown needs to be set off with a large, full bouquet that will move with the dress. Dramatic orchids or lilies are a good accompaniment to figure-hugging or draped silhouettes.

Following the fashion set by the Princess of Wales who carried a very large bouquet, tied bouquets are increasingly popular. It is better not to hold these bouquets directly in front so that the long stems are visible, but instead carry them through the crook of the arm or tied so that the stems make a wheatsheaf shape. For expressive curves and trailing shapes, wired bouquets are still preferable (see p. 108).

FLOWERS FOR THE ATTENDANTS

The same considerations apply when choosing flowers for the bride's attendants. The purpose is to provide unity, either by coordinating colour, design or type of flower and this is especially important if there will be child as well as adult attendants. For adult bridesmaids, the bouquet should be similar in design to the bride's, but smaller and rather less grand.

Above: Flowers for child attendants should be comfortable to wear and easy to manage. Wired circlets are light and flexible; garlands add to the fairytale atmosphere – and are fun to carry!

Left: For a traditional green and white wedding scheme, a little bridesmaid has been given a simple headdress worn low on the side of the head. Ivy wound round her waist adds to the bucolic charm.

Overleaf: Luscious deep red camellias cut low into a glass vase emphasize the romance of a wedding day.

For little bridesmaids, flowers should be less sophisticated, as well as easy to carry. This is a good area to experiment with slightly unusual ideas, as long as you avoid the conspicuously self-conscious. Hoops, pomanders and baskets are fun to carry and add a fairy-tale look to the occasion. A single garland carried by several children can be very pretty.

The groom, ushers and family members can wear buttonholes that coordinate with the flowers in the bridal bouquet. Women can be given corsages using some of the bridal flowers; for men, a rose makes a refreshing change from the ubiquitous carnation.

FLOWERS FOR THE CEREMONY

Although the bride's flowers should provide the basis for the design of all the other floral decorations, wherever the ceremony is held – church, synagogue, registry office – will be the first sight guests have of the main theme. The storyline begins here. Flower displays should be planned to make maximum impact at strategic points, but remember to ask permission before you begin to decorate. If your budget is very limited, remember that it is better to opt for one good-sized arrangement than dot a few flowers around where they will not be noticed.

Entrances are important. You can garland the main doorway or place a large arrangement to one side immediately indoors to welcome the guests. Another key position is at the front of the congregation, where flowers provide a focal point during the service when, for much of the time, the bride and groom will have their backs turned.

Position displays so that they are on the eyeline of guests when seated. Because the arrangements must be effective at a distance, it is particularly important to group species together, emphasizing form. Lilies clustered together have much more impact than single trumpets dotted about in a display.

Pew ends are another natural site for decoration. They can be treated very simply, with posies or small bunches of flowers and ivy tied on with a trailing ribbon. Strewing rose petals or daffodil heads along either side of the

main aisle will make a pathway of colour – buy cheap flowers or those past their best. Petals also make a charming alternative to confetti, and one which is often more welcome. Baskets full of petals can be left waiting by the main door, providing an additional decorative touch during the ceremony.

Right: Roses, ranunculus and hellebores make a vivid St. Valentine's Day posy. The tight, compact shape of the bouquet would work well with a tailored wedding outfit.

FLOWERS FOR THE RECEPTION

Flowers at the reception will gain impact if you keep to the same colour or design theme. Plan displays as for any special occasion or party – a little drama or theatricality never goes amiss. Group species together and keep the arrangements positioned fairly high up, especially in marquees. They should be visible over the heads of a crowd; low-level displays will not be noticed and will only get in the way.

Provide a good welcome in the entrance hall, or wherever guests will be received. This is also likely to be the place where photographs are taken, and where the new couple will eventually take their leave. You can emphasize architectural detail – a stairway or arch – or set a good-sized display on a hall table.

The same themes can be continued in the food area. In the country, even a simple jug of daffodils set on each table can be effective. Drinks or buffet tables can be decorated with garlands, petals or larger displays. It is also a nice touch to edge trays of drinks or canapés with petals or flower heads.

Don't neglect the opportunity to decorate the wedding cake. Cutting the cake is one wedding event which is always commemorated on film and a well-decorated cake makes a good centrepiece. Crown the cake with rosebuds or small flower heads; you can even play up the spring theme with icing of the same colour.

Meadow Bouquet

Bouquets for little bridesmaids should not be too grand or formal. These country-style flowers have been simply bunched together to look like the child has just picked them herself from a spring meadow. The bouquet will last longer than if it were wired, with the stems removed.

FLOWERS AND FOLIAGE

Cornflowers
Pinks
White single chrysanthemums
Cow parsley/Queen Anne's Lace
Buttercups
Ivy

MATERIALS

Twine
Raffia or ribbon

METHOD

1 Select a large flower for the centre. Attach string or twine to the stem, about 7 inches (17.5cm) down from the head. (The distance of the string from the head determines the width of the final bouquet.)
2 Lay another flower at an angle to one side of the central flower and bind in with string.
3 Keep adding the flowers at an angle, binding each one in and rotating the bouquet in your hand.
4 As the bouquet increases, the stems should make a spiral or wheatsheaf shape. Place the more delicate flowers at the edge. Add the ivy last of all.
5 Cover the string or twine with raffia or ribbon. Tie one strand around stems then knot over ready-made bow.

CARE

This type of bouquet should last well all day, and may be replaced in water to revive the flowers.

Bridal Arch

A country church porch has been garlanded in blue and white to greet the bride, picking up the colour of the gate and sundial. The same idea can be adapted to create a floral arch at home, either over the main entrance or an inside doorway. The arch is suspended from masonry nails, but stout picture hangers or meat hooks caught over a ledge or architrave will also work. Always ask permission before decorating a church, inside or out.

FLOWERS AND FOLIAGE

Powdery blue hydrangeas
Purple stocks
White single chrysanthemums
Delphiniums
Dark purple lazianthus
Solomon's seal
Cow parsley/Queen Anne's Lace

MATERIALS

Chicken wire
Blocks of oasis
Wire
Masonry nails, picture
  hangers or meat hooks

METHOD

1 Lay blocks of soaked oasis along a rectangular strip of chicken wire. The size of the chicken wire and oasis should be relative to the size of the finished arch and the thickness of the flower stems.
2 Roll the chicken wire into a sausage shape, with the oasis inside. Secure with wire along the length and at the ends.
3 Attach the roll of oasis and chicken wire around the doorway with nails or hooks.
4 Insert the flower heads into the oasis, building up to a dome shape in cross-section. Angle the heads so that some face down, some ahead and some upwards.

CARE

It is better not to make the arch too much ahead of time; it will be at its best for about a day.

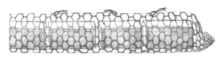

Easter Wedding

This variation on an Easter theme combines lilies, the traditional symbol of purity, with tulips, ivy and humble cow parsley/Queen Anne's Lace for a natural, almost 'wild' look. Wedding displays need to be visible from a distance and the focal point of an arrangement should be level with the eyeline of seated guests.

FLOWERS AND FOLIAGE	MATERIALS
White longiflorum lilies	Oasis
Pink tulips	Plastic lining
Cow parsley/Queen	Water-resistant plastic tape
Anne's lace	Chicken wire
Ivy, jasmine or honeysuckle	Fine wire

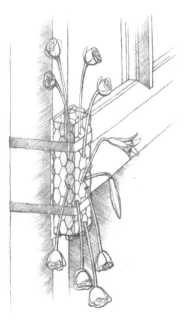

METHOD

1   Before attaching floral decoration to any part of a church's structure, you must ask permission. You may be required to show that you can prevent water damage or be asked to avoid using nails.
2   Cover the back of a piece of soaked oasis with plastic lining and wrap in chicken wire to prevent it from crumbling. Attach the oasis to a convenient spot (in this case the struts of an arch) with water-resistant tape. The plastic backing will prevent water leaking onto the wood.
3   Insert the flowers into the oasis, angling them in an arc, so that some point upwards, some down and some point straight ahead on the eyeline of the congregation. Larger flowers should be placed at the centre to make a focal point.
4   Use trails of ivy, jasmine or honeysuckle to extend the line of the display upwards and downwards, catching the tendrils up with small pieces of fine wire.

CARE

Water the oasis regularly if required for more than one day.

Wedding Cake

Many occasions, such as weddings, christenings, anniversaries and birthdays call for a celebration cake. Often, the cake is a focal point for toasts and picture-taking, so to lend a special touch to such an event it is especially effective to decorate the cake with fresh flowers. Remember when you are displaying a cake on a separate table to consider the whole effect. Tablecloths should reach the floor and watch out for eyesores in the background such as exit signs or radiators.

FLOWERS AND FOLIAGE

Pink and white roses
Rose leaves
Rose petals

MATERIALS

A tiered cake
Plastic lining
Circular piece of oasis,
    about 1½ inches in
    diameter and
    2 inches high (4 × 5cm).

METHOD

1 Cut stems off most of the roses and mass different shades of pink and white around the bases of the tiers, with the emphasis on the lower layer.
2 Soak the oasis and wrap the base in plastic lining so that water does not leak on to the cake.
3 Insert roses around the lower part of the oasis so that just the heads are visible.
4 Build up in the centre of the oasis using roses with longer stems to accentuate the height.
5 Sprinkle rose petals around the tablecloth.

CARE

The topmost arrangement can be taken off and kept for a few days. Water the oasis.

Special Occasions

Left: For an intimate gathering, a delicate table display emphasizes the fragile beauty of an embroidered screen and a cream lace cloth. White jasmine winds around the lamp stand; lilac, pink roses and sections of hydrangea decorate the base.

Flowers instantly suggest a celebration and make a natural accompaniment to any special occasion. Even those who rarely buy flowers for their own enjoyment nearly always feel the need for at least one display at a dinner party or grand event. Flowers also make perfect gifts and, if chosen with care, can reflect the personality of the recipient or express a particular message. Spring festivities – Easter, Passover, St. Valentine's Day, Mother's Day – can suggest floral themes which will add to the enjoyment of a party or special occasion.

Right: Wallflowers are such a common sight in the garden that their potential for display can be overlooked. This flower tree consists of bunches of wallflowers massed in vivid shades for a rich tapestry effect, inserted into a ball of oasis. The trunk is cemented into a pot which is disguised under a layer of bun moss pinned in position.

PARTY FLOWERS

Designing floral displays for a party gives you the opportunity to indulge in a little theatricality. If the party has a theme, the flowers can provide additional emphasis; if not, flowers can always help to create the right mood, express the style of decoration or the type of entertainment.

Don't be afraid to exaggerate. It is important to remember that flowers need to be striking to remain noticeable once a room is filled with people. Small or tentative displays will simply be overlooked. Accordingly, arrangements need to be larger than usual and positioned so that they can be seen. Floor-level displays, for example, are ruled out for cocktail parties or occasions when people will be standing. Also, it is safer to avoid placing large displays on tables in main traffic routes where they can be knocked over all too easily.

When creating a large arrangement, it is important to group species for impact. Individual flower heads do not read well from a distance; three or more clustered together express both colour and form more vividly. Although spring flowers can be angular and sparse, many types are cheap enough to be massed together to create a sense of abundance. Because larger displays are more effective in a party setting, it is often better to create arrangements in oasis in order to achieve flowing shapes.

Before you decide on a design or theme for your party, it is a good idea to sit down and think of everything that reminds you of the occasion. When I am asked to produce a design for a theme party, I let my imagination run riot, and then work back to an idea or image which is expressive but not wildly eccentric. Examples of the kind of ideas and images that Spring conjures up may include: eggs and birds' nests, white candles for a religious occasion, rabbits and chicks for a family party, bulbs and pots to suggest new spring growth. St. Valentine's Day conjures up images of old-fashioned tributes, such as lace hearts, Victorian-style garlands, cards and cupids.

Left: Pedestals do not necessarily demand a tall arrangement; instead they can be treated more like side tables. A low display of ranunculus in hot contrasting colours lead the eye to the view of bright pink cherry blossom.

TABLE SETTINGS

One obvious consideration when designing table displays is that the flowers should not obstruct views. Low, trailing arrangements are better than a high container filled with flowers which will act as an obstacle to conversation. And if the flowers are heavily scented, this will interfere with the appreciation of food and wine.

Spring table settings can be designed to simulate a landscape, with moss, terracotta pots filled with eggs and clumps of bulb flowers. Alternatively, beautiful flower heads, such as lily or amaryllis trumpets can be cut low to provide a table-level focal point.

Do not neglect the opportunity to coordinate flowers and food, especially if food is laid out on a buffet table. Seafood platters or plates of smoked salmon can suggest a pink floral theme; white tulips perfectly complement asparagus spears. More inventively, you can combine flowers, fruit and vegetables in a display. Line a clear glass container with purple cabbage leaves or with fruit slices – kiwis, lemons, oranges and fresh green apples have good cross-sections – and then fill the centre of the container with appropriately coloured flowers. The edges of plates or drinks trays can also be decorated with petals or leaves. But don't use poisonous or inedible berries in a mixed flower and fruit arrangement – your guests may be tempted to sample them.

GIFTS

Flowers are a thoughtful gift; even more so if a little care and consideration has gone into the style of presentation. Although flowers are a good solution in situations where a more personal gift would be inappropriate, this does not mean that they themselves should look impersonal. Even if you are ordering flowers from a florist, by supplying details of the occasion, the style of the house or the personal tastes of the recipient you will make the selection more meaningful.

If you are taking flowers to a dinner party, arrange them in a spiralled or tied bunch so that they are ready to go straight into a vase. The host or hostess will rarely have time to arrange the flowers themselves and a tied bunch is a more spontaneous gesture than giving a display created in oasis.

Tied bunches are also suitable gifts for those in hospital. A posy arrangement in oasis is also a good idea, especially since containers may be in short supply. A display of simple spring flowers arranged in a basket would strike the right note for a new mother and avoid the cliché of a pink or blue theme. But remember to avoid flowers that are very perfumed – in a confined space this can be overpowering.

To mark a special achievement or as a thank-you gift, you can combine flowers with other presents, such as chocolates, champagne or perfume. The style of packaging is often a good starting point. Tie the flowers in with a ribbon so that they become an integral part of the gift. With a little imagination, the results can be memorable: I was once asked to design a bouquet in racing colours; on another occasion, I added scrolls of stave paper to an arrangement for someone who had just passed an important music exam.

Right: The strong vivid shades of this tied posy have a distinctly masculine appeal. Nowadays, many men enjoy receiving flowers, especially if the selection reflects their favourite colours.

St. Valentine's Day

To mark a special occasion, especially one with such traditional associations as St. Valentine's Day, it is a good idea to pick a theme and play it up to the hilt. Red roses mean true love and an arrangement in the style of a Victorian posy makes a charming table setting. Unseasonal though they are, strawberries are naturally heart-shaped; and to complete the theme, red wine is the perfect accompaniment to a romantic dinner for two.

FLOWERS AND FOLIAGE

Red roses (open)
Miniature red rosebuds
Bun moss
Ivy leaves
Strawberries

MATERIALS

Two white plates
Glass candlestick
Oasis
Cocktail sticks

METHOD

1   Slice the strawberries in half to emphasize their heart shape. Place the slices in layers on a plate, to form a heart shape. Trim the edge of the plate with half-strawberries and rosebuds.
2   Fill the base of a glass candlestick with water and rest an open rose on it.
3   To make the posy, cut a block of oasis to fit within a plate. Group a cluster of open roses at the top. Surround the top "posy" with a 2 inch (5 cm) border of moss, leaving about 1 inch (2 cm) at the bottom.
4   Work around the base of the oasis, making a regular pattern of three roses alternating with three strawberries. Insert cocktail sticks into the oasis to secure the strawberries.
5   Insert washed ivy leaves into the oasis and on the plate. Then add clusters of miniature rosebuds.

CARE

Water the oasis regularly.

Easter Lily

The cool, pure beauty of longiflorum lilies and their characteristic fluted shape inspired this Easter table decoration. Extravagantly, the lily trumpets are split, petals wrapped around a wine glass and laid around the circumference of a plate. The result, although not long-lasting, is a memorable and evocative setting for a special occasion.

FLOWERS AND FOLIAGE

White double tulips
Longiflorum lilies
Tulip leaf

MATERIALS

Fluted wine glass
Matching dessert and dinner plate
Double-sided tape

METHOD

1   Cut the lilies at the base of the flower, open out and remove the stamens.
2   Wrap the lily petals around the base of a wine glass, covering the ragged lower edges with a tulip leaf. Secure the leaf in place with double-sided tape.
3   Fill the glass with water and add a bunch of double tulips.
4   Decorate the edge of a dinner plate with lily petals. Lay a dessert plate on top to hold the petals in place.

CARE

The split lily flowers will only last the course of the meal.

Family Easter Table

On Easter Day, a special table decoration can add to the enjoyment of the family celebration. This spring garden arrangement, with its half-concealed treasure of eggs, would be fun to make with the children. Instead of quails' eggs in the little terracotta pots, you could substitute sugar or chocolate ones.

FLOWERS AND FOLIAGE	MATERIALS
Cherry blossom	Quails' eggs
Apple blossom	Three small saucers
Muscari	Three small blocks of oasis
Primroses	Hairpins or fine wire
Anemones	Terracotta pots
Bun moss	
Sphagnum moss	
Ivy	

METHOD

1. Space three saucers along the length of the table and place a block of soaked oasis in each.
2. Cover the oasis with flowers, clustering species together like a garden scene. Start at the ends and work to the centre.
3. Pile bun moss and sphagnum moss between the saucers to create the effect of a landscape.
4. Rest the terracotta pots in the centre, on their sides, banking with moss to keep them stable. Insert flowers and eggs into the pots.
5. Break up the line of the display with ivy tendrils, winding in between place settings, if desired.

CARE

Water oasis regularly. Spray moss with water to prevent it from drying out – but take care not to ruin the table's finish. Display will last several days.

Indoor Topiary

A rather architectural decoration for a side table or buffet, these clipped box shapes would lend a touch of theatricality to a party. Inspired by a *trompe l'oeil* which was itself an imitation of a real formal garden, the topiary is a way of bringing the outdoors in. The shapes can be left to dry out and then sprayed green so that they can be used again.

FLOWERS AND FOLIAGE

Large branches of box, cut at least 2½ inches (6 cm) long

MATERIALS

Oasis or chicken wire
Garden shears

METHOD

1 Remove the leaves from the base of the box branches.
2 Either crumple sections of chicken wire into the desired shapes or cut pieces of oasis to shape.
3 Push clumps of box into the chicken wire or oasis. Density is important.
4 Clip the topiary so that the planes are even and sharp.

CARE

Leave to dry out. Spray green if used again.

Christening

Blue is prevalent in the spring palette, which makes an appropriate colour theme for a christening of a baby boy. The colour, however, can be hard to manage in dark churches, almost disappearing where light is dim. To decorate a font, light blue hydrangeas are massed low for impact and the darker shade of blue trachelium reserved for background depth. Hydrangeas cover large areas well so are best used low down, with daintier flowers towards the edges.

FLOWERS AND FOLIAGE

Cornflowers
Hydrangeas
Stocks
Trachelium
Solomon's seal
Ivy

MATERIALS

Plastic trays
Standard-sized oasis blocks

METHOD

1 Lay plastic trays around the base of the font and fill with soaked oasis blocks.
2 Insert hydrangea heads and clusters of stocks low down, with trachelium pushed in for background depth.
3 Make several gatherings of taller, more delicate flowers, such as cornflowers, around the circumference, to break up the line. Allow Solomon's seal to arc over so that the tiny bell flowers are visible.
4 Insert ivy so that it trails across the floor. Scatter stock and cornflower petals on the edge of the font.

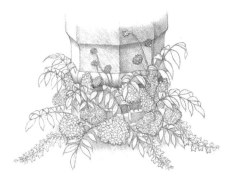

CARE

As the arrangement is in oasis, it can be prepared the day before, or first thing in the morning.

Mother's Day Posy

True Victorian posies were arranged in rings of colour and flower type. For this Mother's Day bouquet, the traditional notion has been simplified, using two evocative spring flowers, bound together and tied with a vivid ribbon. Whatever the occasion, this type of tied bunch makes an ideal gift and is ready to be put straight into a vase.

FLOWERS AND FOLIAGE

Gelda rose
Narcissi
Bluebells
Salaal leaves

MATERIALS

Ribbon
Twine

METHOD

1   Mass the narcissi together in one hand, making a dome shape.
2   Add on the bluebells one by one, rotating the bouquet in your hand.
3   Place gelda roseheads between the bluebells.
4   Add the foliage, making a neat border.
5   Secure the stems with twine and cover with a ribbon.

CARE

Put into water as soon as possible.

Lily Crown

Table centres should be low enough that guests can look over them and they are often most effective when they reflect the colours and style of decoration of their surroundings. In this case the predominantly green colour scheme and chenille tablecloth suggested a matching arrangement, which is also faintly nostalgic to suit the atmosphere of the room. The double lily theme – arums with lily-of-the-valley within – makes an intriguing focal point.

FLOWERS AND FOLIAGE

Arum lilies
Lily-of-the-valley
Bun moss

MATERIALS

Green dish
Oasis
Water vials
Hairpins or wire

METHOD

1   Place a piece of oasis in the centre of the bowl and insert three arum lilies in the centre of the oasis to make a crown.
2   Insert arum lilies lower down, facing outwards.
3   Lay lily-of-the-valley leaves, with clusters of lily-of-the-valley inside, at the base of the arrangement.
4   Fill small vials with water and insert into the topmost arum trumpets. Place lily-of-the-valley in the vials, so that they appear over the top of the arums.
5   Pin moss around the flowers to hide patches of oasis.

CARE

Top up the water in the bowl to keep oasis moist. Check the level of water in the vials regularly.

Floral Tapestry

A grand occasion often calls for a rich, abundant display, especially if the setting is equally impressive. But this is the type of arrangement which can be difficult to create with relatively sparse spring flowers. Here, the depth of colour in an antique hanging and the intricate decoration of a carved sideboard are set off by a tumbling cascade. The basic design is the traditional "front-facing" arrangement, but the flowers have been allowed to flow down over the side of the chest, echoing the scrolled carving.

FLOWERS AND FOLIAGE

Lilac
Red and orange parrot tulips
Cherry blossom
Euphorbia
Arum lilies
Forget-me-nots
Variegated ivy
Cow parsley/Queen Anne's Lace
Lilac leaves
Silver birch leaves

MATERIALS

Large low bowl, about
  10 inches across and
  3 inches deep
  (25 × 8 cm)
Squares of oasis
Saucer
Small piece of oasis

METHOD

1 Fill the bowl with the pieces of soaked oasis, so that the oasis stands to a height of about 8 inches (20 cm) above the top of the container.
2 Start by building height in the centre, inserting clusters of flowers and foliage.
3 Work forward from the back of the oasis, leaving only one-third of the oasis without flowers. Although the arrangement is designed to be viewed from the front, this distribution avoids a stiff, flat edge and aids balance.
4 Insert tulips to one side. Allowing them to curl down over the edge by inserting the stems upwards at an angle.
5 Arrange darker flowers – purple lilac and red tulips – in soaked oasis placed in a small saucer. Set this display in the centre of the sideboard. Add ivy tendrils.

CARE

Water daily. After being filled with oasis, the container should still allow for a reservoir of water.

possible to avoid recutting and thus prevent the sap from flowing freely. But if you do need to trim the stems, cut them under running water to wash excess sap away. Add a proprietary plant food to the flower water to help neutralize the effect.

Roses

Most roses come wrapped in cellophane and the heads may have wilted or dropped slightly by the time you get them home. Remove the cellophane and take off the thorns from the stems so that the flowers are more comfortable to work with. Trim the stems (they do not need to be hammered) and dip them into 2 inches (5 cm) of boiling water for 20 seconds to clear any airblocks. Then wrap the flowers in tissue paper or newspaper and place in deep water for two hours. Some of the foliage can be left on the stems to aid water absorption.

Tulips

To straighten floppy or limp tulips, wrap tightly in a tube of tissue paper or newspaper and place in a bucket of deep water for two hours.

Violets

Wilted violets can be revived by completely immersing flowers and stems in water for 15 to 30 minutes.

Azaleas

Wilted azaleas in pots can be revived by submerging the pot – not the entire plant – in water. Wait until bubbles have stopped coming to the surface. The flowers will return to normal but the leaves will remain hanging at an angle.

WATER

Cool water will prolong the life of cut flowers. In some circumstances, however, you may wish to place the flowers in warm water to open buds and bring on the display ahead of time.

The water should be as deep as the container allows. The crucial relationship is between the length of the stem

and depth of the water: the longer the stem, the deeper the water should be. Long-stemmed flowers in shallow containers will last a fraction of their normal lifespan.

Water is an alien medium for flowers; stems drown and decompose, depositing particles which change the chemical nature of the water. To slow down the process of decay, take off the foliage below the water line and change the water in containers as frequently as possible, retrimming the stems by ½ inch (1 cm) at each water change. You can also add a flower food to the water which will make the flowers last longer, but this does yellow the water. With flower food, you can change the water every three to four days; without, allow only one or two days between changes. Stock stems decay particularly quickly, making the water foul. Stock water should be changed once a day.

One of the problems of needing to change the water frequently is that you run the risk of disturbing a carefully composed and balanced arrangement. If the flowers are all in good condition, you can stand the vase or container under the tap and leave the water running until it has come up over the side. But if some of the flowers are beginning to brown, changing the water provides an opportunity to discard dead and dying heads. In mixed arrangements, some species will last longer than others and this is a good way of gaining maximum value and enjoyment. Similarly, flowers in bud can be arranged in a tall, elegant container; once opened, they can be cut down and arranged in a lower vase to display the heads prominently.

Always clean containers thoroughly between use. Use bleach or a washing-up liquid and scour to remove the tidemark of algae and scum. Dirty containers only speed up the process of decay.

TEMPERATURE

It is important not to overheat flowers, especially when they are out of water. If possible, visit the florist last when you are out shopping – don't leave flowers baking on the back seat of a car while you run other errands.

Positioning is also important, especially for spring

flowers. Naturally warm places — sunny window sills, near radiators, above or alongside working fireplaces — will cause flowers to spoil quickly. Very draughty locations such as hearths and doorways can also cause problems to some varieties.

If you need to take flowers on a journey, pack them in a box and add a synthetic ice pack to keep them cool and fresh. The flowers should not touch the ice pack.

USING OASIS

Oasis or florist's foam consists of a green porous material, which is available in pyramid, square and cylindrical shapes as well as the standard blocks 12 × 6 × 4 inches (30 × 15 × 10 cm). Although some people maintain that oasis promotes an artificial, contrived look, it can be used to create natural-looking arrangements and is extremely useful for deep or awkwardly shaped containers. Oasis may also be the only means of creating certain shapes, such as those where flowers spill down over the edge of the container.

In some ways, oasis is a more "natural" medium for flowers than water. Oasis supports the stem in the same manner as earth or a branch. It holds a certain amount of water and presents it to the plant in the same way as earth: the flower draws as much water as it needs. Despite these advantages, flowers generally do not last as long in oasis as they do in water due to limited stem length inserted.

The size and shape of the oasis will depend on the arrangement, container, and the quantity and size of stems. For a display where you want the flowers to flow down over the edge of the container, the block or blocks of oasis must stand far enough above the top of the container that stems can be inserted at an upward angle. Oasis is easy to cut; odd shapes can be built up by covering blocks with chicken wire. Chicken wire wrapped around oasis will also prevent it from crumbling excessively; this is especially advisable for large arrangements where many stems are being inserted.

After the oasis has been cut to size, it should be soaked. Float the block on top of a sink or bucket of

Right: For weddings, the pew ends are traditional places for floral decorations. Both the design and the flowers must be robust enough to withstand accidental knocks, yet not encroach on the guests' view. Take care when attaching displays to church fixtures — and always ask permission.

water. The oasis will become saturated in a matter of minutes. Do not push the oasis down to submerge it as this will cause air blocks and dry areas will remain inside.

Before you begin an arrangement, think about which direction you want the flowers to fall. Mentally divide the oasis in sections and insert the flowers in the relevant portion. Avoid crossing stems. A haphazard approach will create problems: the display will lack stability and the oasis will be more likely to break up.

Insert each stem by holding it low down and feeding it into the oasis. Do not try to insert the flower by pushing down from the head – the stem may buckle or even break. You need to insert at least 1½ or 2 inches (4-5 cm) of stem into the oasis so that the flower has a good chance of absorbing water. Some stems, such as those of daffodils and narcissi, are difficult to insert and you may have to make a hole first with a pointed tool.

The oasis should sit in a container filled with water. Top up the level daily, pouring water over the oasis as well as into the container. If the oasis is allowed to dry out, it is difficult to restore the necessary capillary action. Flower heads can be sprayed with a plant water spray. Oasis cannot be reused, but it is very cheap and widely available.

CHICKEN WIRE

Chicken wire is standard florist's equipment and has many varied uses. If a large arrangement needs to be transported, chicken wire wrapped around the oasis will prevent it from crumbling. Chicken wire also makes a good alternative to oasis for creating large vase displays. The wire should be crumpled and tangled so that the flowers remain stable.

Chicken wire also allows you to use a few flowers, or flowers with fine stems, in a wide-necked container. If the container is opaque, a ball of chicken wire pushed down inside will hold the flowers in place. For a glass container, you can lay a mesh of chickenwire over the neck and arrange the flowers within the grid. The wire can be disguised with moss. (Alternatively, you can construct the grid with tape.)

Left: Two large arrangements of spring flowers – daffodils and narcissi – crown the newel posts of a stairway, with garlands flowing down beside the balustrade, altogether a dramatic entrance for a bride. Since such displays require a considerable quantity of flowers, selecting cheaper and more plentiful seasonal varieties makes good economic sense.

WATER VIALS

Water vials, test tubes or "thimbles" are small glass containers of the type which are often seen enclosing the stems of orchids. They are available in about four different sizes to suit different stems. The special advantage of vials is that they allow cut flowers to be combined with potted displays. The vial is inserted in the earth or basket to hold water for the cut flowers, foliage or trails. The vial must be in an upright position and topped up daily with water. For a large arrangement, a small jam jar makes a good alternative.

WIRING

Wiring flowers consists of removing the stems and attaching lightweight wire to the flower head. The technique is mostly used for making wedding bouquets and headdresses, and for dried flower arrangements. Time-consuming, intricate, and demanding quite different skills from those used in flower arranging, wiring is best left to the professionals, especially for such important occasions as weddings.

Many people believe that wiring inevitably results in a stiff, unnatural-looking bouquet, but such rigid constructions are merely poor examples of the technique. It is perfectly possible to wire flowers so that they retain a sense of movement and fluidity. The great advantage of wiring is that it is possible to create trailing or curving shapes. And because the stems are removed, bouquets are considerably lighter and more comfortable to carry, and headdresses are easier to wear for long periods.

The wire must be strong enough to support the flower, but not rigid. There are over twenty gauges of wire, from fine silver for wiring tiny hyacinth bells to heavier steel for attaching large amaryllis heads. In a bouquet, individual wires are drawn together and taped with special florist's tape to make a comfortable handle.

The florist will be able to advise as to which flowers are suitable for wired bouquets or headdresses. The loss of stem inevitably shortens the life of flowers and certain species, such as anemones, snowdrops or narcissi will not survive for long periods once the stems are removed.

Right: Wedding flowers are special – and they must be right. Wiring, in particular, is a job for the professional and should not be attempted by the amateur.

Index

Numbers in italics refer to photographs

Acknowledgements

With special thanks to Liz Wilhide, Di Lewis, Kirsty Craven, Paul Morgan and the wonderful team at Pavilion Books, who have made working on this book such fun.

To all who have allowed me to ransack their homes for 'the sake of art', and to everyone slaving away at 56 James Street, without whom this book would have been impossible.

To Amy and Lucy for creating havoc as sweet bridesmaids, and to all my family for their never-ending support.

To Linda Smith for the fabulous 'palette' illustrations, and to Gill Elsbury for the delightful line illustrations.

Jane Packer

The Publishers gratefully acknowledge the following for providing locations for photography:
  Rev. and Mrs J. Beech, Ellingham Church near
    Ringwood, Hampshire
  Gillian and Peter Catto, London
  Jim and Ingrid Kempston, Ashford, Kent
  Stan Morse, Shillingford, Oxfordshire
  Carl and Pia Sandeman, Petworth, Sussex